Books by Volker Heide

No More Tears

God's Punch Line

The Key is Love

Let Go and Let God

Bless the Lord, O My Soul

Available on Amazon

In Paperback and Kindle

BLESS THE LORD, O MY SOUL

STUDIES IN THE PSALMS

Volker Heide

King of Kings Publishing
Madison, Connecticut

BLESS THE LORD, O MY SOUL

STUDIES IN THE PSALMS

Preface

This book is a Bible Study that looks at selected Psalms. It is meant to lead you deeper into the Word of God. You will need a Bible to look up the passages that are discussed for each Psalm.

Every Psalm is printed out before the discussion. They are all taken from the classic King James Version. Questions are included for reflection and prayer. Let these Psalms guide you to a better understanding of our gracious God. They will speak to your deepest needs and strengthen your faith in Christ.

Each verse of every Psalm is worthy of careful study. The more you read them, the more powerful they become. The discussions are only an introduction to each Psalm. They are designed to help you better understand the message God wants to communicate to you.

However, the best way to study the Psalms is to simply read them slowly and carefully. Think about each line. Reflect upon each single verse.

Read them over and over again. Open your heart to what the Holy Spirit is saying to you through his Word.

Notice also, how the New Testament quotes many of the Psalms to show how Jesus is the promised Messiah and King of Israel. Christ is the Savior that God promised to the Old Testament saints. The Psalms point us to the Son of God.

The Psalms also help us to worship our Lord with joy and thanksgiving. They inspire us and give us courage and hope, especially during times of suffering and heartache. Sometimes we do not know what we should say in our prayers. Here, the Psalms can teach you how to approach God with confidence and certainty.

May God richly bless you as you study the Psalms and all of the Scriptures! "Bless the LORD, O my soul: and all that is within me, bless his holy name. Bless the LORD, O my soul, and forget not all his benefits." Amen!

I will extol thee, my God, O king; and I will bless thy name for ever and ever.

Every day will I bless thee; and I will praise thy name for ever and ever.

Great is the LORD, and greatly to be praised; and his greatness is unsearchable.

One generation shall praise thy works to another, and shall declare thy mighty acts.

I will speak of the glorious honour of thy majesty, and of thy wondrous works.

Psalm 145

BLESS THE LORD, O MY SOUL

STUDIES IN THE PSALMS

Featuring

Psalm 1: The Two Ways

1 Blessed is the man that walketh not in the counsel of the ungodly, nor standeth in the way of sinners, nor sitteth in the seat of the scornful.

2 But his delight is in the law of the LORD; and in his law doth he meditate day and night.

3 And he shall be like a tree planted by the rivers of water, that bringeth forth his fruit in his season; his leaf also shall not wither; and whatsoever he doeth shall prosper.

4 The ungodly are not so: but are like the chaff which the wind driveth away.

5 Therefore the ungodly shall not stand in the judgment, nor sinners in the congregation of the righteous.

6 For the LORD knoweth the way of the righteous: but the way of the ungodly shall perish.

Psalm 1: The Two Ways

This is a wisdom Psalm and it serves as a preface to the entire book of Psalms. It speaks of two ways - the way of God and the way of unbelief. The way of God includes meditating on the Word of God, delighting in God's wisdom and putting the Word into practice. The way of unbelief mocks the Word and rejects God's promises. True wisdom always builds upon the foundation of the Bible.

Read Matthew 7:24-29 to see how Jesus compares his teaching to a foundation of rock. The Lord Jesus presents us with the two ways of Psalm 1. Putting God's Word into practice is always the way to go.

Jesus says, "Enter through the narrow gate. For wide is the gate and broad is the road that leads to destruction, and many enter it. But small is the gate and narrow the road that leads to life, and only a few enter it."

Read 1 Corinthians 1:18-2:5 to discover how Christ is the wisdom and power of God. Paul says that the crucified Christ is the true wisdom we should seek. "The foolishness of God is wiser than man's wisdom, and the weakness of God is stronger than man's strength." Notice especially 1 Corinthians 2:4-5. God's power is revealed through his Word.

As you study the Psalms, follow the road of God's wisdom and walk in his ways. Open your mind to the power and beauty of God's Word. Read the Bible every day and explore the Scriptures with the attitude of faith and trust. Pray for the Holy Spirit to enlighten you and teach you.

Then, you will enter the small gate and travel down the narrow road of God's Word. You will be richly blessed as you learn to apply the Psalms to your life each day.

"Blessed is the man that walketh not in the counsel of the ungodly, nor standeth in the way of sinners, nor sitteth in the seat of the scornful. But his delight is in the law of the LORD; and in his law doth he meditate day and night."

Psalm 2: Thou Art My Son

1   Why do the heathen rage, and the people imagine a vain thing?

2   The kings of the earth set themselves, and the rulers take counsel together, against the LORD, and against his anointed, saying,

3   Let us break their bands asunder, and cast away their cords from us.

4   He that sitteth in the heavens shall laugh: the Lord shall have them in derision.

5   Then shall he speak unto them in his wrath, and vex them in his sore displeasure.

6   Yet have I set my king upon my holy hill of Zion.

7   I will declare the decree: the LORD hath said unto me, Thou art my Son; this day have I begotten thee.

8   Ask of me, and I shall give thee the heathen for thine inheritance, and the uttermost parts of the earth for thy possession.

⁹ Thou shalt break them with a rod of iron; thou shalt dash them in pieces like a potter's vessel.

¹⁰ Be wise now therefore, O ye kings: be instructed, ye judges of the earth.

¹¹ Serve the LORD with fear, and rejoice with trembling.

¹² Kiss the Son, lest he be angry, and ye perish from the way, when his wrath is kindled but a little. Blessed are all they that put their trust in him.

Psalm 2: Thou Art My Son

This is a Messianic Psalm. It is frequently quoted in the New Testament, where it is repeatedly applied to the Lord Jesus. He is the Son who is installed by God the Father to be King over all the earth. Jesus is the Anointed One. "Anointed" means "Christ" (in Greek) or "Messiah" (in Hebrew).

The position of Psalm 2 at the very beginning of the book of Psalms alerts us to the Messianic quality of all of the following Psalms.

In this Psalm, we see how God's Messiah encounters much opposition and rejection from the unbelieving world. Yet, in the end, God's purposes are accomplished through his Anointed One. Therefore, everyone should now hail the Son of God as King of Kings and Lord of Lords.

See Acts 4:23-31 and Acts 13:32-41 to discover how Psalm 2 is fulfilled in our Lord Jesus Christ. In Acts 4, we see how the apostles apply Psalm 2 the events of Good Friday. In Acts 13, Paul applies Psalm 2 to the resurrection of Christ. Carefully notice how the apostles proclaim the good news of salvation in Jesus Christ, the Son of God.

Psalm 2 also appears at our Lord's baptism by John, and on the Mount of Transfiguration when Christ revealed his glory to his disciples. The Book of Revelation will also quote this Psalm to show how the Risen Lord now rules his church and protects us.

In verse 6, God the Father says, "I have set my King on Zion, my holy hill." This leads us to the events of Good Friday on a holy hill outside of Jerusalem, where our Lord was set upon a cross and crucified. Our King will wear a crown of thorns and die for our sins. Jesus dies as "The King of the Jews."

However, as we see in the readings from Acts, the Messiah is victorious in the end as he rises from the dead on Easter morning. Our King is vindicated and exalted by the Father.

Reflect upon the Lord's victory and what it means for you today. Think about how the apostles used the Psalms to show us that Jesus is the Son of God and the Savior of the world. "Therefore, kiss the Son and put your trust in him."

Psalm 6: When Your Soul is Vexed

1 O LORD, rebuke me not in thine anger, neither chasten me in thy hot displeasure.

2 Have mercy upon me, O LORD; for I am weak: O LORD, heal me; for my bones are vexed.

3 My soul is also sore vexed: but thou, O LORD, how long?

4 Return, O LORD, deliver my soul: oh save me for thy mercies' sake.

5 For in death there is no remembrance of thee: in the grave who shall give thee thanks?

6 I am weary with my groaning; all the night make I my bed to swim; I water my couch with my tears.

7 Mine eye is consumed because of grief; it waxeth old because of all mine enemies.

8 Depart from me, all ye workers of iniquity; for the LORD hath heard the voice of my weeping.

9 The LORD hath heard my supplication; the LORD will receive my prayer.

10 Let all mine enemies be ashamed and sore vexed: let them return and be ashamed suddenly.

Psalm 6: When Your Soul is Vexed

This is a prayer for mercy when your soul is in anguish. Many Psalms are prayers for help and deliverance. They honestly confess our weakness and the pain we feel. "I am weary with my groaning." However, these Psalms also rely on God's grace and mercy. Our hope is in the Lord and in his deliverance

Read John 12:20-36 to see the anguish of Jesus as he speaks about his impending death on the cross. Our Lord will be lifted up on the cross to bring us eternal help and deliverance. He will give himself for us and will experience our pain and distress.

How does the suffering and death of Jesus give you comfort in times of trouble? Which specific verses in Psalm 6 best express your need right now? Which verses express your faith in Christ? Write them out on a note card to keep and memorize.

Read this Psalm carefully when your soul is vexed and when you feel like there is no hope. Make these words your own by praying them aloud. "The Lord hath heard my supplication; he will receive my prayer."

Psalm 8: How Excellent is Thy Name

1 O LORD our Lord, how excellent is thy name in all the earth! who hast set thy glory above the heavens.

2 Out of the mouth of babes and sucklings hast thou ordained strength because of thine enemies, that thou mightest still the enemy and the avenger.

3 When I consider thy heavens, the work of thy fingers, the moon and the stars, which thou hast ordained;

4 What is man, that thou art mindful of him? and the son of man, that thou visitest him?

5 For thou hast made him a little lower than the angels, and hast crowned him with glory and honour.

6 Thou madest him to have dominion over the works of thy hands; thou hast put all things under his feet:

7 All sheep and oxen, yea, and the beasts of the field;

8 The fowl of the air, and the fish of the sea, and whatsoever passeth through the paths of the seas.

9 O LORD our Lord, how excellent is thy name in all the earth!

Psalm 8: How Excellent is Thy Name

This Psalm gives praise to the Creator of the universe. God is the Maker of heaven and earth. All things were made by his power and wisdom. "How excellent is thy name in all the earth!"

When you consider the beauty and complexity of creation, you realize that a Divine Intelligence stands behind it all. Verse 3 especially marvels at the stars and vast galaxies God created. Verse 4 contemplates God's gift of human life. Verses 6-8 looks at how God entrusted the care of his creation to humanity.

Adam and Eve were created in the image of God so that they might have direct fellowship with their Creator and be caretakers of this world. We know that their rebellion ruined the perfect relationship we had with God in the beginning. As a result, sin and death entered God's perfect world.

Read Hebrews 2:5-18 to see how God the Father sends his Son to become flesh and blood like us. The Son comes to redeem lost sinners and to restore a lost creation.

We marvel that our Lord became a real human being like us so that he might save us from sin, death and the power of the devil. The Son of God suffered death on our behalf so that he might restore what we had lost. "How excellent is thy name in all the earth!"

Read Psalm 8 aloud and join David in praising God for the gift of life, creation and everything else we see around us. Marvel at God artistic design. Give thanks for the beauty of the heavens and the earth.

Psalm 16: I Shall Not Be Moved

1 Preserve me, O God: for in thee do I put my trust.

2 O my soul, thou hast said unto the LORD, Thou art my Lord: my goodness extendeth not to thee;

3 But to the saints that are in the earth, and to the excellent, in whom is all my delight.

4 Their sorrows shall be multiplied that hasten after another god: their drink offerings of blood will I not offer, nor take up their names into my lips.

5 The LORD is the portion of mine inheritance and of my cup: thou maintainest my lot.

6 The lines are fallen unto me in pleasant places; yea, I have a goodly heritage.

7 I will bless the LORD, who hath given me counsel: my reins also instruct me in the night seasons.

8 I have set the LORD always before me: because he is at my right hand, I shall not be moved.

9 Therefore my heart is glad, and my glory rejoiceth: my flesh also shall rest in hope.

10 For thou wilt not leave my soul in hell; neither wilt thou suffer thine Holy One to see corruption.

11 Thou wilt show me the path of life: in thy presence is fulness of joy; at thy right hand there are pleasures for evermore.

Psalm 16: I Shall Not Be Moved

This Psalm rejoices that God is present in our daily life. Every day, we walk with the Lord by faith. He is at our right hand, guiding and protecting us. We have the confidence that the Lord is with us all the way through this earthly life, and even beyond to the day of resurrection and life everlasting. Because of God's presence, we can be strong and courageous, even in the face of suffering. "Because he is at my right hand, I shall not be moved."

Reads Acts 2:22-36 to see how Peter uses this Psalm on the Day of Pentecost to proclaim the resurrection of Christ. Peter shows how the Holy One of God was raised from the dead for us and our salvation.

Psalm 16 ends with the promise of life after death, a promise fulfilled in the resurrection and ascension of Jesus. "Thou wilt show me the path of life: in thy presence is fulness of joy; at thy right hand there are pleasures for evermore."

Our Lord Jesus truly is the King of Kings and the Ruler of all creation. How does this comfort you? How can you use Psalm 16 to help you in times of trouble and heartache?

Reflect upon the fact that because Christ lives, you too shall live. "We are more than conquers through him who loved us." "If God is for us, who can be against us?"

Make these words your very own today: "I have set the LORD always before me: because he is at my right hand, I shall not be moved."

Psalm 19: The Heavens Declare the Glory of God

1 The heavens declare the glory of God; and the firmament showeth his handywork.

2 Day unto day uttereth speech, and night unto night showeth knowledge.

3 There is no speech nor language, where their voice is not heard.

4 Their line is gone out through all the earth, and their words to the end of the world. In them hath he set a tabernacle for the sun,

5 Which is as a bridegroom coming out of his chamber, and rejoiceth as a strong man to run a race.

6 His going forth is from the end of the heaven, and his circuit unto the ends of it: and there is nothing hid from the heat thereof.

7 The law of the LORD is perfect, converting the soul: the testimony of the LORD is sure, making wise the simple.

8   The statutes of the LORD are right, rejoicing the heart: the commandment of the LORD is pure, enlightening the eyes.

9   The fear of the LORD is clean, enduring for ever: the judgments of the LORD are true and righteous altogether.

10   More to be desired are they than gold, yea, than much fine gold: sweeter also than honey and the honeycomb.

11   Moreover by them is thy servant warned: and in keeping of them there is great reward.

12   Who can understand his errors? Cleanse thou me from secret faults.

13   Keep back thy servant also from presumptuous sins; let them not have dominion over me: then shall I be upright, and I shall be innocent from the great transgression.

14   Let the words of my mouth, and the meditation of my heart, be acceptable in thy sight, O LORD, my strength, and my redeemer.

Psalm 19: The Heavens Declare the Glory of God

In this Psalm, we hear that all of creation proclaims that there is a Creator. God's glory is reflected in the beauty of creation, in the sky, stars and sun. They all declare the majesty of the Maker of heaven and earth. The beauty and design of creation point to a Creator. "The heavens declare the glory of God; and the firmament showeth his handywork."

In the same way, the written Word reveals the power and the glory of God. God's revelation in the Scriptures points us to the way that leads to life, salvation and true wisdom.

The Word also leads us to repentance, confession of sin, forgiveness and renewal. "Who can understand his errors? cleanse thou me from secret faults." The Word always leads us to Jesus the Messiah. He is the Way and the Truth and the Life. In him, we find the hope we all need.

Read Romans 8:18-27 to discover the future hope that awaits us. The Holy Spirit shows us the glory of the new creation to come. In this life, we groan and are weighed down by the burdens of life, but we look forward to the day when God will make all things new. Then, there will be no more tears, suffering or death. "I consider that our present sufferings are not worth comparing with the glory that will be revealed in us."

Read Revelation 21:1-5 to catch glimpse of the new creation to come. Note especially 21:4-5. Write these verses down on a card and read them often. God promises us, "I am making everything new!'

Reflect upon the fact that we can look to the future with hope and confidence. We know that the Almighty God who made all things is in control of everything, including our life.

God's Word reminds us of God's promises. "The law of the LORD is perfect, converting the soul: the testimony of the LORD is sure, making wise the simple."

Psalm 22: The Psalm of the Passion

1 My God, my God, why hast thou forsaken me? why art thou so far from helping me, and from the words of my roaring?

2 O my God, I cry in the daytime, but thou hearest not; and in the night season, and am not silent.

3 But thou art holy, O thou that inhabitest the praises of Israel.

4 Our fathers trusted in thee: they trusted, and thou didst deliver them.

5 They cried unto thee, and were delivered: they trusted in thee, and were not confounded.

6 But I am a worm, and no man; a reproach of men, and despised of the people.

7 All they that see me laugh me to scorn: they shoot out the lip, they shake the head, saying,

8 He trusted on the LORD that he would deliver him: let him deliver him, seeing he delighted in him.

9 But thou art he that took me out of the womb: thou didst make me hope when I was upon my mother's breasts.

10 I was cast upon thee from the womb: thou art my God from my mother's belly.

11 Be not far from me; for trouble is near; for there is none to help.

12 Many bulls have compassed me: strong bulls of Bashan have beset me round.

13 They gaped upon me with their mouths, as a ravening and a roaring lion.

14 I am poured out like water, and all my bones are out of joint: my heart is like wax; it is melted in the midst of my bowels.

15 My strength is dried up like a potsherd; and my tongue cleaveth to my jaws; and thou hast brought me into the dust of death.

16 For dogs have compassed me: the assembly of the wicked have enclosed me: they pierced my hands and my feet.

17 I may tell all my bones: they look and stare upon me.

18 They part my garments among them, and cast lots upon my vesture.

19 But be not thou far from me, O LORD: O my strength, haste thee to help me.

20 Deliver my soul from the sword; my darling from the power of the dog.

21 Save me from the lion's mouth: for thou hast heard me from the horns of the unicorns.

22 I will declare thy name unto my brethren: in the midst of the congregation will I praise thee.

23 Ye that fear the LORD, praise him; all ye the seed of Jacob, glorify him; and fear him, all ye the seed of Israel.

24 For he hath not despised nor abhorred the affliction of the afflicted; neither hath he hid his face from him; but when he cried unto him, he heard.

25 My praise shall be of thee in the great congregation: I will pay my vows before them that fear him.

26 The meek shall eat and be satisfied: they shall praise the LORD that seek him: your heart shall live for ever.

27 All the ends of the world shall remember and turn unto the LORD: and all the kindreds of the nations shall worship before thee.

28 For the kingdom is the LORD'S: and he is the governor among the nations.

29 All they that be fat upon earth shall eat and worship: all they that go down to the dust shall bow before him: and none can keep alive his own soul.

30 A seed shall serve him; it shall be accounted to the Lord for a generation.

31 They shall come, and shall declare his righteousness unto a people that shall be born, that he hath done this.

Psalm 22: The Psalm of the Passion

This is a remarkable Psalm. No other Psalm points beyond itself so fully. It leads us directly to the events that took place on Good Friday. Our Lord Jesus will directly quote this Psalm as he hangs upon the cross suffering for the sins of the world.

David wrote this Psalm about 1,000 years before Christ. As David describes the suffering and persecution he experienced (especially under King Saul and during Absalom's rebellion), he gives us a powerful prophetic look at the ultimate suffering of God's Messiah.

"My God, my God, why hast thou forsaken me? why art thou so far from helping me, and from the words of my roaring?"

"All they that see me laugh me to scorn: they shoot out the lip, they shake the head, saying, He trusted on the LORD that he would deliver him: let him deliver him, seeing he delighted in him."

"I am poured out like water, and all my bones are out of joint: my heart is like wax; it is melted in the midst of my bowels."

"My strength is dried up like a potsherd; and my tongue cleaveth to my jaws; and thou hast brought me into the dust of death."

"For dogs have compassed me: the assembly of the wicked have enclosed me: they pierced my hands and my feet."

"I may tell all my bones: they look and stare upon me."

"They part my garments among them, and cast lots upon my vesture."

Read Matthew 27:33-56 to see how Christ is crucified. He is pierced in his hands and feet. He is mocked by the crowds. He is forsaken by the Father as he suffers our punishment. Christ took our place and became our substitute.

For three hours, a total darkness covered the land. That was when the Son of God endured hell and damnation. He was forsaken and cut off from God the Father. He pays the price for our sins, which is eternal damnation. He suffered the curse of hell so that we might be set free and forgiven.

"God made him who had no sin to be sin for us, so that in him we might become the righteousness of God."

"Christ redeemed us from the curse of the law by becoming a curse for us, for it is written, 'Cursed is everyone hung on a tree.'"

"He himself bore our sins in his body on the tree, so that we might die to sins and live for righteousness. By his wounds, you have been healed."

Also, read John 19:17-37 to see how this Psalm and many other Bible prophecies are fulfilled by Christ. Notice the reference to "I thirst" ("My tongue cleaveth to my jaws; and thou hast brought me into the dust of death"), and the soldiers dividing the garments of Jesus ("They part my garments among them, and cast lots upon my vesture.")

Verses 22-31 describe God's final deliverance of his suffering servant. We are now called to praise God's redemption and his saving work. The Father accepts the Messiah's suffering. At the end of our Lord's passion, he cried out, "It is finished," and "Into your hands, O Father, I commit my spirit."

Notice how Psalm 22 ends with a note of triumph and celebration. "For he hath not despised nor abhorred the affliction of the afflicted; neither hath he hid his face from him; but when he cried unto him, he heard."

The resurrection of Christ will show how the Messiah has done everything necessary so that we might receive salvation. Therefore, we praise our Savior and glorify his name.

"They shall come, and shall declare his righteousness unto a people that shall be born, that he hath done this."

Read again this great Psalm and reflect upon each verse. Think about how the Lord suffered for us. Pray the Lord's Prayer for a closing to your devotional today.

Psalm 23: Our Good Shepherd

1 The LORD is my shepherd; I shall not want.

2 He maketh me to lie down in green pastures: he leadeth me beside the still waters.

3 He restoreth my soul: he leadeth me in the paths of righteousness for his name's sake.

4 Yea, though I walk through the valley of the shadow of death, I will fear no evil: for thou art with me; thy rod and thy staff they comfort me.

5 Thou preparest a table before me in the presence of mine enemies: thou anointest my head with oil; my cup runneth over.

6 Surely goodness and mercy shall follow me all the days of my life: and I will dwell in the house of the LORD for ever.

Psalm 23: Our Good Shepherd

In Psalm 23, we confidently confess our faith in our Good Shepherd. David, who wrote this Psalm, was a shepherd when he was young. Therefore, he was quite familiar with this occupation. He knew what was required for the proper care of sheep such as good pasture, clean water, protection and care.

David mentions green pastures, still waters and God restoring our soul. He also speaks of being led in the paths of righteousness.

The Lord walks with us through the dark valleys of this life. He prepares a table for us (Holy Communion) and anoints us with oil (Holy Baptism). "Surely goodness and mercy shall follow me all the days of my life: and I will dwell in the house of the LORD for ever."

Read John 10:11-18. Notice how our Good Shepherd lays down his life for his sheep. Christ dies for sheep who love to wander. Our Lord does everything necessary so that the words of Psalm 23 might come true for us.

Now read John 10:27-30. You are safe in those hands that were nailed to the cross. No one can snatch you out of the hands of the Good Shepherd.

What are your favorite verses from these two readings from John 10? Write them down on a card and read them each day this week.

Psalm 24: Lift Up Your Heads

1 The earth is the LORD'S, and the fulness thereof; the world, and they that dwell therein.

2 For he hath founded it upon the seas, and established it upon the floods.

3 Who shall ascend into the hill of the LORD? or who shall stand in his holy place?

4 He that hath clean hands, and a pure heart; who hath not lifted up his soul unto vanity, nor sworn deceitfully.

5 He shall receive the blessing from the LORD, and righteousness from the God of his salvation.

6 This is the generation of them that seek him, that seek thy face, O Jacob.

7 Lift up your heads, O ye gates; and be ye lift up, ye everlasting doors; and the King of glory shall come in.

8 Who is this King of glory? The LORD strong and mighty, the LORD mighty in battle.

9 Lift up your heads, O ye gates; even lift them up, ye everlasting doors; and the King of glory shall come in.

10 Who is this King of glory? The LORD of hosts, he is the King of glory.

Psalm 24: Lift Up Your Heads

This Psalm speaks of worshipping the God of all creation. We are able to approach a holy and righteous God only because our sins have been forgiven in Christ. "This is the generation of them that seek him, that seek thy face, O Jacob."

See Hebrews 4:14-5:10 to discover how Jesus, our High Priest, has opened the way to God for us. Because of Christ, we can now approach God with confidence and joy.

Psalm 24 also describes how the King of Glory comes to dwell in his house. When we worship together, God is truly present to bless and save us. "He shall receive the blessing from the LORD, and righteousness from the God of his salvation."

Note the majestic description of the King of Glory. He is "The LORD, strong and mighty," "The LORD of hosts," and "The One mighty in battle."

Our God is great and awesome. He has infinite power and wisdom. God is the Creator of all things and everything belongs to him. "The earth is the LORD'S, and the fulness thereof; the world, and they that dwell therein."

The good news today is that the all-powerful King of Glory comes to us in grace. He forgives us our sins for the sake of Christ. He comes to us in love, mercy and compassion. Therefore, seek his face and ascend to the hill of the Lord. Worship your King with gladness and joy. Rejoice that you belong to him.

Psalm 25: Remember Not the Sins of My Youth

1 Unto thee, O LORD, do I lift up my soul.

2 O my God, I trust in thee: let me not be ashamed, let not mine enemies triumph over me.

3 Yea, let none that wait on thee be ashamed: let them be ashamed which transgress without cause.

4 Show me thy ways, O LORD; teach me thy paths.

5 Lead me in thy truth, and teach me: for thou art the God of my salvation; on thee do I wait all the day.

6 Remember, O LORD, thy tender mercies and thy lovingkindnesses; for they have been ever of old.

7 Remember not the sins of my youth, nor my transgressions: according to thy mercy remember thou me for thy goodness' sake, O LORD.

8 Good and upright is the LORD: therefore will he teach sinners in the way.

9 The meek will he guide in judgment: and the meek will he teach his way.

10 All the paths of the LORD are mercy and truth unto such as keep his covenant and his testimonies.

11 For thy name's sake, O LORD, pardon mine iniquity; for it is great.

12 What man is he that feareth the LORD? him shall he teach in the way that he shall choose.

13 His soul shall dwell at ease; and his seed shall inherit the earth.

14 The secret of the LORD is with them that fear him; and he will show them his covenant.

15 Mine eyes are ever toward the LORD; for he shall pluck my feet out of the net.

16 Turn thee unto me, and have mercy upon me; for I am desolate and afflicted.

17 The troubles of my heart are enlarged: O bring thou me out of my distresses.

18 Look upon mine affliction and my pain; and forgive all my sins.

19 Consider mine enemies; for they are many; and they hate me with cruel hatred.

20 O keep my soul, and deliver me: let me not be ashamed; for I put my trust in thee.

21 Let integrity and uprightness preserve me; for I wait on thee.

22 Redeem Israel, O God, out of all his troubles.

Psalm 25: Remember Not the Sins of My Youth

Psalm 25, like so many of the Psalms, appeals to God's mercy for help and deliverance. We all experience times of difficulty and heartache. We all struggle through life and sometimes our troubles seem endless. Yet, with God's help, we can be reassured that we have the promise of life and forgiveness.

In this Psalm, we cry out, "Unto thee, O LORD, do I lift up my soul. O my God, I trust in thee." We pray, "Remember not the sins of my youth, nor my transgressions: according to thy mercy remember thou me for thy goodness' sake, O LORD." We cry out, "For thy names sake, O LORD, pardon mine iniquity; for it is great."

Notice especially the honesty of verses 16-22. This is a prayer for when you feel overwhelmed by your troubles.

Read Luke 15:11-32 for the story of a young man who learned the hard way this lesson of Psalm 25. Give thanks that even though you were once dead, now you are alive. Though you were once lost; now you are found.

With God, there is always hope! We can always return to the Father who will welcome us back with open arms. For the sake of the Son, the Father always forgives sinners. Now, we can learn to follow God's way. "Good and upright is the LORD; therefore he will teach sinners in the way."

Psalm 27: The Lord is My Light and My Salvation

1 The LORD is my light and my salvation; whom shall I fear? the LORD is the strength of my life; of whom shall I be afraid?

2 When the wicked, even mine enemies and my foes, came upon me to eat up my flesh, they stumbled and fell.

3 Though an host should encamp against me, my heart shall not fear: though war should rise against me, in this will I be confident.

4 One thing have I desired of the LORD, that will I seek after; that I may dwell in the house of the LORD all the days of my life, to behold the beauty of the LORD, and to inquire in his temple.

5 For in the time of trouble he shall hide me in his pavilion: in the secret of his tabernacle shall he hide me; he shall set me up upon a rock.

6 And now shall mine head be lifted up above mine enemies round about me: therefore will I offer in his tabernacle sacrifices of joy; I will sing, yea, I will sing praises unto the LORD.

7 Hear, O LORD, when I cry with my voice: have mercy also upon me, and answer me.

8 When thou saidst, Seek ye my face; my heart said unto thee, Thy face, LORD, will I seek.

9 Hide not thy face far from me; put not thy servant away in anger: thou hast been my help; leave me not, neither forsake me, O God of my salvation.

10 When my father and my mother forsake me, then the LORD will take me up.

11 Teach me thy way, O LORD, and lead me in a plain path, because of mine enemies.

12 Deliver me not over unto the will of mine enemies: for false witnesses are risen up against me, and such as breathe out cruelty.

13 I had fainted, unless I had believed to see the goodness of the LORD in the land of the living.

14 Wait on the LORD: be of good courage, and he shall strengthen thine heart: wait, I say, on the LORD.

Psalm 27: The Lord is My Light and My Salvation

This is a favorite Psalm of many people. This is a triumphant affirmation of confidence and hope, even in the face of great suffering. We know that if God is on our side, we have nothing to fear. Note especially verses 4-5, 7-8 and 13-14. Read them again slowly and reflect upon these words.

Truly, "The Lord is my light and my salvation; whom shall I fear? The Lord is the strength of my life; of whom shall I be afraid?" Read Romans 8:28-39 to see how nothing can separate you for the love of God in Christ. We are more than conquerors through him who loved us!

Knowing that God loves us leads us to worship him with joy and gladness. Worship should be the highpoint of our week as we give thanks to our gracious Lord.

"One thing have I desired of the LORD, that will I seek after; that I may dwell in the house of the LORD all the days of my life, to behold the beauty of the LORD, and to inquire in his temple."

"When thou saidst, Seek ye my face; my heart said unto thee, Thy face, LORD, will I seek."

When we seek God's face, we are able to be of good courage. We can have a sure and certain hope knowing that God will strengthen us through his grace in Christ. "Hear, O LORD, when I cry with my voice: have mercy also upon me, and answer me."

Psalm 32: Blessed is He Whose Transgression is Forgiven

1 Blessed is he whose transgression is forgiven, whose sin is covered.

2 Blessed is the man unto whom the LORD imputeth not iniquity, and in whose spirit there is no guile.

3 When I kept silence, my bones waxed old through my roaring all the day long.

4 For day and night thy hand was heavy upon me: my moisture is turned into the drought of summer.

5 I acknowledged my sin unto thee, and mine iniquity have I not hid. I said, I will confess my transgressions unto the LORD; and thou forgavest the iniquity of my sin.
Selah

6 For this shall every one that is godly pray unto thee in a time when thou mayest be found: surely in the floods of great waters they shall not come nigh unto him.

7 Thou art my hiding place; thou shalt preserve me from trouble; thou shalt compass me about with songs of deliverance.

8 I will instruct thee and teach thee in the way which thou shalt go: I will guide thee with mine eye.

9 Be ye not as the horse, or as the mule, which have no understanding: whose mouth must be held in with bit and bridle, lest they come near unto thee.

10 Many sorrows shall be to the wicked: but he that trusteth in the LORD, mercy shall compass him about.

11 Be glad in the LORD, and rejoice, ye righteous: and shout for joy, all ye that are upright in heart.

Psalm 32: Blessed is He Whose Transgression is Forgiven

This is a "penitential Psalm," a Psalm of confession and absolution. After we sincerely confess our sins to God, we are ready to hear that word of absolution, which says, "For the sake of Jesus Christ, the Son of God, your sins are forgiven!"

A powerful spiritual healing takes place in such a sincere repentance. Read verses 3-5 aloud. It is good to honestly confess your sins to God. Pray for his healing help. "Therefore, let everyone who is godly pray to you."

Note how verses 1-2 are used by Paul to demonstrate that we are saved by grace through faith in Christ. Read Romans 4:1-8 and reflect upon the power of God's forgiveness.

"I acknowledged my sin unto thee, and mine iniquity have I not hid. I said, I will confess my transgressions unto the LORD; and thou forgavest the iniquity of my sin." "He that trusteth in the LORD, mercy shall compass him about. Be glad in the LORD, and rejoice, ye righteous: and shout for joy, all ye that are upright in heart."

Psalm 34: O Taste and See That the Lord is Good

1 I will bless the LORD at all times: his praise shall continually be in my mouth.

2 My soul shall make her boast in the LORD: the humble shall hear thereof, and be glad.

3 O magnify the LORD with me, and let us exalt his name together.

4 I sought the LORD, and he heard me, and delivered me from all my fears.

5 They looked unto him, and were lightened: and their faces were not ashamed.

6 This poor man cried, and the LORD heard him, and saved him out of all his troubles.

7 The angel of the LORD encampeth round about them that fear him, and delivereth them.

8 O taste and see that the LORD is good: blessed is the man that trusteth in him.

9 O fear the LORD, ye his saints: for there is no want to them that fear him.

10 The young lions do lack, and suffer hunger: but they that seek the LORD shall not want any good thing.

11 Come, ye children, hearken unto me: I will teach you the fear of the LORD.

12 What man is he that desireth life, and loveth many days, that he may see good?

13 Keep thy tongue from evil, and thy lips from speaking guile.

14 Depart from evil, and do good; seek peace, and pursue it.

15 The eyes of the LORD are upon the righteous, and his ears are open unto their cry.

16 The face of the LORD is against them that do evil, to cut off the remembrance of them from the earth.

17 The righteous cry, and the LORD heareth, and delivereth them out of all their troubles.

18 The LORD is nigh unto them that are of a broken heart; and saveth such as be of a contrite spirit.

¹⁹ Many are the afflictions of the righteous: but the LORD delivereth him out of them all.

²⁰ He keepeth all his bones: not one of them is broken.

²¹ Evil shall slay the wicked: and they that hate the righteous shall be desolate.

²² The LORD redeemeth the soul of his servants: and none of them that trust in him shall be desolate.

Psalm 34: O Taste and See That the Lord is Good

This is a Psalm of praise to the Lord for deliverance and answer to prayer. God hears us when we call to him in times of trouble. That is why we seek refuge in our God and Savior. Here is the true wisdom of God.

"The righteous cry, and the LORD heareth, and delivereth them out of all their troubles. The LORD is nigh unto them that are of a broken heart; and saveth such as be of a contrite spirit."

Peter quotes this Psalm extensively in his First Letter. Peter reminds us, that if we have "tasted" God's goodness, we will follow God's way of wisdom.

Read 1 Peter 2:1-3 and 3:8-12. Peter tells us that we should seek to live in harmony with others. Show compassion and humility to all. Follow the way of Christ.

"Keep thy tongue from evil, and thy lips from speaking guile. Depart from evil, and do good; seek peace, and pursue it."

Now read 1 Peter 2:21-25. How does the suffering of Christ during his passion help you to deal with the troubles you face? Reflect upon what the Lord has suffered for you. Let his love truly touch your heart and soul.

"O taste and see that the LORD is good: blessed is the man that trusteth in him."

Psalm 46: A Mighty Fortress is Our God

1 God is our refuge and strength, a very present help in trouble.

2 Therefore will not we fear, though the earth be removed, and though the mountains be carried into the midst of the sea;

3 Though the waters thereof roar and be troubled, though the mountains shake with the swelling thereof.

4 There is a river, the streams whereof shall make glad the city of God, the holy place of the tabernacles of the most High.

5 God is in the midst of her; she shall not be moved: God shall help her, and that right early.

6 The heathen raged, the kingdoms were moved: he uttered his voice, the earth melted.

7 The LORD of hosts is with us; the God of Jacob is our refuge.

8 Come, behold the works of the LORD, what desolations he hath made in the earth.

⁹ He maketh wars to cease unto the end of the earth; he breaketh the bow, and cutteth the spear in sunder; he burneth the chariot in the fire.

¹⁰ Be still, and know that I am God: I will be exalted among the heathen, I will be exalted in the earth.

¹¹ The LORD of hosts is with us; the God of Jacob is our refuge.

Psalm 46: A Mighty Fortress is Our God

This Psalm speaks of having a strong faith, even when the whole world seems to be falling apart. Creation itself may be coming apart at the seams, but God is still in control. When our life comes unglued, God is our refuge and strength. He is our fortress and castle in times of sorrow, confusion and fear. We are safe in his presence.

That is why we turn to God in times of trouble. "God is our refuge and strength, a very present help in trouble. Therefore will not we fear, though the earth be removed, and though the mountains be carried into the midst of the sea."

Notice the refrain, "The Lord Almighty is with us; the God of Jacob is our refuge." Martin Luther based his famous hymn, "A Mighty Fortress is our God," on this Psalm. Both Luther's hymn and our Psalm express a confident trust in God's presence and protection.

Read John 14:23-27 and pray that God would surround you with his protection and care. Remember: "The Lord Almighty is with you!" Therefore, do not be afraid, but trust in God's power and grace.

Psalm 51: Create in Me a Clean Heart

1 Have mercy upon me, O God, according to thy lovingkindness: according unto the multitude of thy tender mercies blot out my transgressions.

2 Wash me thoroughly from mine iniquity, and cleanse me from my sin.

3 For I acknowledge my transgressions: and my sin is ever before me.

4 Against thee, thee only, have I sinned, and done this evil in thy sight: that thou mightest be justified when thou speakest, and be clear when thou judgest.

5 Behold, I was shapen in iniquity; and in sin did my mother conceive me.

6 Behold, thou desirest truth in the inward parts: and in the hidden part thou shalt make me to know wisdom.

7 Purge me with hyssop, and I shall be clean: wash me, and I shall be whiter than snow.

8 Make me to hear joy and gladness; that the bones which thou hast broken may rejoice.

9 Hide thy face from my sins, and blot out all mine iniquities.

10 Create in me a clean heart, O God; and renew a right spirit within me.

11 Cast me not away from thy presence; and take not thy holy spirit from me.

12 Restore unto me the joy of thy salvation; and uphold me with thy free spirit.

13 Then will I teach transgressors thy ways; and sinners shall be converted unto thee.

14 Deliver me from bloodguiltiness, O God, thou God of my salvation: and my tongue shall sing aloud of thy righteousness.

15 O Lord, open thou my lips; and my mouth shall show forth thy praise.

16 For thou desirest not sacrifice; else would I give it: thou delightest not in burnt offering.

¹⁷ The sacrifices of God are a broken spirit: a broken and a contrite heart, O God, thou wilt not despise.

¹⁸ Do good in thy good pleasure unto Zion: build thou the walls of Jerusalem.

¹⁹ Then shalt thou be pleased with the sacrifices of righteousness, with burnt offering and whole burnt offering: then shall they offer bullocks upon thine altar.

Psalm 51: Create in Me a Clean Heart

Psalm 51 is David's humble prayer for forgiveness. David had fallen into adultery, deception, lying and murder. Yet, in the end, there was forgiveness for King David. He honestly confessed his sin and received mercy.

"For I acknowledge my transgressions: and my sin is ever before me. Against thee, thee only, have I sinned, and done this evil in thy sight: that thou mightest be justified when thou speakest, and be clear when thou judgest."

Every verse of this Psalm is worthy of careful study. Especially note verses 1-6. Try to imagine how David prayed verses 10-12.

Now, make the words of this Psalm your own by praying them aloud. Consider your own situation in life right now, and reflect upon God's mercy in Christ.

Read 1 John 1:5-10 and see how God creates a pure heart within us through the blood of Christ. In Jesus, we are forgiven and receive the Holy Spirit. The joy of salvation fills our hearts.

"Create in me a clean heart, O God; and renew a right spirit within me. Cast me not away from thy presence; and take not thy holy spirit from me. Restore unto me the joy of thy salvation; and uphold me with thy free spirit."

Psalm 67: Cause His Face to Shine on Us

1 God be merciful unto us, and bless us; and cause his face to shine upon us;

2 That thy way may be known upon earth, thy saving health among all nations.

3 Let the people praise thee, O God; let all the people praise thee.

4 O let the nations be glad and sing for joy: for thou shalt judge the people righteously, and govern the nations upon earth.

5 Let the people praise thee, O God; let all the people praise thee.

6 Then shall the earth yield her increase; and God, even our own God, shall bless us.

7 God shall bless us; and all the ends of the earth shall fear him.

Psalm 67: Cause His Face to Shine on Us

This is a missionary Psalm. We pray that all people may come to experience God's peace. "Let the people praise thee, O God; let all the people praise thee." Note especially the beautiful words of verses 1-2.

Read Numbers 6:22-27 to discover the priestly blessing the Lord gave to Moses and Aaron to put upon God's people. The face of God shining upon us is a picture of God's blessing bestowed. "God be merciful unto us, and bless us; and cause his face to shine upon us."

This priestly blessing from Numbers 6 is the same benediction we use to close our worship services. We pray that God would bless us so that we can share his blessing with all people. "The Lord look upon you with favor, and give you peace."

Read 2 Corinthians 13:11-14 to discover another benediction from St. Paul. Pray that the blessing of the Triune God would extend to all people. Pray for the salvation of those you know, your friends and family. Pray that all people may come to experience the wondrous peace and blessing God gives in Christ.

Psalm 73: Guide Me With Thy Counsel

1 Truly God is good to Israel, even to such as are of a clean heart.

2 But as for me, my feet were almost gone; my steps had well nigh slipped.

3 For I was envious at the foolish, when I saw the prosperity of the wicked.

4 For there are no bands in their death: but their strength is firm.

5 They are not in trouble as other men; neither are they plagued like other men.

6 Therefore pride compasseth them about as a chain; violence covereth them as a garment.

7 Their eyes stand out with fatness: they have more than heart could wish.

8 They are corrupt, and speak wickedly concerning oppression: they speak loftily.

9 They set their mouth against the heavens, and their tongue walketh through the earth.

10 Therefore his people return hither: and waters of a full cup are wrung out to them.

11 And they say, How doth God know? and is there knowledge in the most High?

12 Behold, these are the ungodly, who prosper in the world; they increase in riches.

13 Verily I have cleansed my heart in vain, and washed my hands in innocency.

14 For all the day long have I been plagued, and chastened every morning.

15 If I say, I will speak thus; behold, I should offend against the generation of thy children.

16 When I thought to know this, it was too painful for me;

17 Until I went into the sanctuary of God; then understood I their end.

18 Surely thou didst set them in slippery places: thou castedst them down into destruction.

19 How are they brought into desolation, as in a moment! they are utterly consumed with terrors.

20 As a dream when one awaketh; so, O Lord, when thou awakest, thou shalt despise their image.

21 Thus my heart was grieved, and I was pricked in my reins.

22 So foolish was I, and ignorant: I was as a beast before thee.

23 Nevertheless I am continually with thee: thou hast holden me by my right hand.

24 Thou shalt guide me with thy counsel, and afterward receive me to glory.

25 Whom have I in heaven but thee? and there is none upon earth that I desire beside thee.

26 My flesh and my heart faileth: but God is the strength of my heart, and my portion for ever.

27 For, lo, they that are far from thee shall perish: thou hast destroyed all them that go a whoring from thee.

28 But it is good for me to draw near to God: I have put my trust in the Lord GOD, that I may declare all thy works.

Psalm 73: Guide Me With Thy Counsel

This is a wisdom Psalm. It reflects upon the question: "Why do evil people prosper, while the people of God suffer so much?" The Old Testament saints often asked that question. Life was very difficult for God's people back then.

However, Psalm 73 points us to the ultimate outcome on the last day. Judgment awaits those who reject God's way. Evil will be dealt with in the end. But those who live by faith will be blessed by God. "But it is good for me to draw near to God: I have put my trust in the Lord God, that I may declare all thy works."

Psalm 73 reminds us that God is always in control, no matter how things appear right now. Read Hebrews 11:1-40 to discover some real heroes of the faith.

Give thanks for the witness of all the saints who have gone before us. Learn from their example of faith as they dealt with all the trials and tribulations they faced. Remember how St. Paul said, "We must go through many hardships to enter the kingdom of God."

Psalm 84: From Strength to Strength

1 How amiable are thy tabernacles, O LORD of hosts!

2 My soul longeth, yea, even fainteth for the courts of the LORD: my heart and my flesh crieth out for the living God.

3 Yea, the sparrow hath found an house, and the swallow a nest for herself, where she may lay her young, even thine altars, O LORD of hosts, my King, and my God.

4 Blessed are they that dwell in thy house: they will be still praising thee.
Selah

5 Blessed is the man whose strength is in thee; in whose heart are the ways of them.

6 Who passing through the valley of Baca make it a well; the rain also filleth the pools.

7 They go from strength to strength, every one of them in Zion appeareth before God.

8 O LORD God of hosts, hear my prayer: give ear, O God of Jacob.

9 Behold, O God our shield, and look upon the face of thine anointed.

10 For a day in thy courts is better than a thousand. I had rather be a doorkeeper in the house of my God, than to dwell in the tents of wickedness.

11 For the LORD God is a sun and shield: the LORD will give grace and glory: no good thing will he withhold from them that walk uprightly.

12 O LORD of hosts, blessed is the man that trusteth in thee.

Psalm 84: From Strength to Strength

In Psalm 84, we hear a prayer of longing for God's house. We long to draw near to the Lord in worship. "My soul longeth, yea, even fainteth for the courts of the LORD: my heart and my flesh crieth out for the living God."

Blessed are those who worship God every chance they get. "For the LORD God is a sun and shield: the LORD will give grace and glory: no good thing will he withhold from them that walk uprightly."

We seek, in the words of "The Church's One Foundation," that "mystic sweet communion" with our God and Savior. When we worship our Savior, faith is created and sustained. We are nourished and strengthened by God's Word and Sacraments. We receive God's gifts of grace. "They go from strength to strength, every one of them in Zion appeareth before God."

Read Matthew 11:25-30 to see how the Son of God invites us to come into his presence to receive his wondrous blessing. Enter his rest through faith. Experience his peace and blessing. "O LORD of hosts, blessed is the man that trusteth in thee."

Psalm 90: Teach Us to Number Our Days

1 Lord, thou hast been our dwelling place in all generations.

2 Before the mountains were brought forth, or ever thou hadst formed the earth and the world, even from everlasting to everlasting, thou art God.

3 Thou turnest man to destruction; and sayest, Return, ye children of men.

4 For a thousand years in thy sight are but as yesterday when it is past, and as a watch in the night.

5 Thou carriest them away as with a flood; they are as a sleep: in the morning they are like grass which groweth up.

6 In the morning it flourisheth, and groweth up; in the evening it is cut down, and withereth.

7 For we are consumed by thine anger, and by thy wrath are we troubled.

8 Thou hast set our iniquities before thee, our secret sins in the light of thy countenance.

9 For all our days are passed away in thy wrath:
    we spend our years as a tale that is told.

10 The days of our years are threescore years and
    ten; and if by reason of strength they be
    fourscore years, yet is their strength labour
    and sorrow; for it is soon cut off, and we fly
    away.

11 Who knoweth the power of thine anger? even
    according to thy fear, so is thy wrath.

12 So teach us to number our days, that we may
    apply our hearts unto wisdom.

13 Return, O LORD, how long? and let it repent
    thee concerning thy servants.

14 O satisfy us early with thy mercy; that we may
    rejoice and be glad all our days.

15 Make us glad according to the days wherein
    thou hast afflicted us, and the years wherein
    we have seen evil.

16 Let thy work appear unto thy servants, and thy
    glory unto their children.

¹⁷ And let the beauty of the LORD our God be upon us: and establish thou the work of our hands upon us; yea, the work of our hands establish thou it.

Psalm 90: Teach Us to Number Our Days

This is a prayer that the holy and eternal God would have compassion on his suffering people. Many Psalms honestly depict the sorrow and heartache we experience in this fallen world. Life is often dismal and melancholy, especially when our loved ones die and pass away.

"The days of our years are threescore years and ten; and if by reason of strength they be fourscore years, yet is their strength labour and sorrow; for it is soon cut off, and we fly away."

Yet, Psalm 90 directs us to the holy and eternal God who has compassion upon his servants. God has mercy upon his frail people.

"O satisfy us early with thy mercy; that we may rejoice and be glad all our days." Because of Christ, God's favor rests upon us and he "establishes the work of our hands."

The hymn, "O God, Our Help in Ages Past," is based upon this Psalm. As you read this hymn, you can see how Psalm 90 becomes a beautiful prayer of faith. Many great hymns are based squarely on the Psalms.

Read Matthew 6:25-34 to see how our Lord Jesus directs us to God's providence and care.

Jesus says, "Therefore do not worry about tomorrow, for tomorrow will worry about itself. Each day has enough trouble of its own."

"So teach us to number our days, that we may apply our hearts unto wisdom." Amen!

Psalm 91: On Eagles' Wings

1 He that dwelleth in the secret place of the most High shall abide under the shadow of the Almighty.

2 I will say of the LORD, He is my refuge and my fortress: my God; in him will I trust.

3 Surely he shall deliver thee from the snare of the fowler, and from the noisome pestilence.

4 He shall cover thee with his feathers, and under his wings shalt thou trust: his truth shall be thy shield and buckler.

5 Thou shalt not be afraid for the terror by night; nor for the arrow that flieth by day;

6 Nor for the pestilence that walketh in darkness; nor for the destruction that wasteth at noonday.

7 A thousand shall fall at thy side, and ten thousand at thy right hand; but it shall not come nigh thee.

8 Only with thine eyes shalt thou behold and see the reward of the wicked.

9 Because thou hast made the LORD, which is my
   refuge, even the most High, thy habitation;

10 There shall no evil befall thee, neither shall any
   plague come nigh thy dwelling.

11 For he shall give his angels charge over thee, to
   keep thee in all thy ways.

12 They shall bear thee up in their hands, lest thou
   dash thy foot against a stone.

13 Thou shalt tread upon the lion and adder: the
   young lion and the dragon shalt thou trample
   under feet.

14 Because he hath set his love upon me, therefore
   will I deliver him: I will set him on high,
   because he hath known my name.

15 He shall call upon me, and I will answer him: I
   will be with him in trouble; I will deliver him,
   and honour him.

16 With long life will I satisfy him, and show him
   my salvation.

Psalm 91: On Eagles' Wings

This Psalm is a glowing testimony to the security of those who trust in God. Our Lord protects us in our daily life from harm and danger (more than we will ever know or realize). "He who dwells in the shelter of the Most High will rest in the shadow of the Almighty. I will say of the Lord, 'He is my refuge and my fortress, my God, in whom I trust.'"

The hymn, "On Eagles' Wings," is based on Psalm 91. "And he will raise you up on eagles' wings, bear you on the breath of dawn, make you to shine like the sun, and hold you in the palm of his hand." Note especially verses 14-16 of our Psalm. Write these verses on a card and memorize them.

The fact that God watches over and protects his people was misused by the devil to tempt Jesus in the wilderness. Read Matthew 4:1-11, and notice how the devil quotes from Psalm 91. What exactly is the temptation the devil is offering to our Lord? How would this apply to us?

Our Lord was victorious over the devil. He was obedient to the Father and did not give in to the devil's temptations. Read Philippians 2:1-11 to see how our attitude should be the same as

Christ. The Son of God humbled himself and was obedient to the Father all the way to the cross.

Because of Christ, God shows us his salvation and he satisfies us with eternal life. We now have his promise that he will watch over us and carry us on eagles' wings. "I will say of the LORD, He is my refuge and my fortress: my God; in him will I trust."

Psalm 96: Sing Unto the Lord a New Song

1 O sing unto the LORD a new song: sing unto the LORD, all the earth.

2 Sing unto the LORD, bless his name; show forth his salvation from day to day.

3 Declare his glory among the heathen, his wonders among all people.

4 For the LORD is great, and greatly to be praised: he is to be feared above all gods.

5 For all the gods of the nations are idols: but the LORD made the heavens.

6 Honour and majesty are before him: strength and beauty are in his sanctuary.

7 Give unto the LORD, O ye kindreds of the people, give unto the LORD glory and strength.

8 Give unto the LORD the glory due unto his name: bring an offering, and come into his courts.

⁹ O worship the LORD in the beauty of holiness: fear before him, all the earth.

¹⁰ Say among the heathen that the LORD reigneth: the world also shall be established that it shall not be moved: he shall judge the people righteously.

¹¹ Let the heavens rejoice, and let the earth be glad; let the sea roar, and the fulness thereof.

¹² Let the field be joyful, and all that is therein: then shall all the trees of the wood rejoice

¹³ Before the LORD: for he cometh, for he cometh to judge the earth: he shall judge the world with righteousness, and the people with his truth.

Psalm 96: Sing Unto the Lord a New Song

Psalm 96 is a call to all nations to praise the Lord as the only true God and to proclaim the glory of his reign throughout the world. Here is an Old Testament anticipation of the world mission of the New Testament people of God. "O sing unto the LORD a new song: sing unto the LORD, all the earth. Sing unto the LORD, bless his name; show forth his salvation from day to day. Declare his glory among the heathen, his wonders among all people."

Notice also how all of creation is called upon to praise the Lord God. One day, all creatures will rejoice in God's righteous rule over a renewed heaven and earth. God will make all things new and this includes the entire universe and everything that exists within it, including plants, animals, oceans, the atmosphere, stars and galaxies. "Behold, I make all things new!"

This is the joyful message of hope we are to proclaim to everyone. "Let the heavens rejoice, and let the earth be glad; let the sea roar, and the fulness thereof. Let the field be joyful, and all that is therein: then shall all the trees of the wood rejoice."

Read Matthew 28:16-20 to discover how the Risen Lord calls for us to go forth into the entire world to make disciples of all nations. "Sing to the Lord, praise his name; proclaim his salvation day after day."

In Christ, we are able to sing a new song of salvation. It is the song of his cross, resurrection and ascension. We worship our Savior in the beauty of his holiness. "Give unto the LORD, O ye kindreds of the people, give unto the LORD glory and strength." "O worship the LORD in the beauty of holiness: fear before him, all the earth."

Pray that all people may come to know the one true God. Share the joyful message of hope that you have in Christ. Reach out and share the gift you have received. "Go and make disciples of all nations."

Psalm 100: Make a Joyful Noise

1 Make a joyful noise unto the LORD, all ye lands.

2 Serve the LORD with gladness: come before his presence with singing.

3 Know ye that the LORD he is God: it is he that hath made us, and not we ourselves; we are his people, and the sheep of his pasture.

4 Enter into his gates with thanksgiving, and into his courts with praise: be thankful unto him, and bless his name.

5 For the LORD is good; his mercy is everlasting; and his truth endureth to all generations.

Psalm 100: Make a Joyful Noise

Psalm 100 is a short but memorable Psalm. This is a classic call to praise the Lord. We were created to worship the Lord with gladness and joy. This is the God who made us. We are his! "We are his people, and the sheep of his pasture."

We enter God's house with thanksgiving as we praise his holy name. "For the LORD is good, his mercy is everlasting; and his truth endureth to all generations."

Read Luke 2:25-40 to see how Simeon and Anna entered God's house to worship the baby Jesus, God's Messiah. They were filled with joy when they saw God's promised Savior.

Give thanks that God has enabled you to recognize that Jesus is the promised Messiah. "Be thankful unto him, and bless his name."

Reflect upon the fact that you belong to the Lord; your life is in his hands. God loves you and promises to bless you with his mercy and truth.

Read Psalm 100 again and notice how verse 3 is the center of its message. Verses 2 and 4 parallel each other as they describe our worship, and verses 1 and 5 show us the object of our worship, the Lord God who is good and merciful.

Therefore, "Enter into his gates with thanksgiving, and into his courts with praise: be thankful unto him, and bless his name. For the LORD is good; his mercy is everlasting; and his truth endureth to all generations." Amen!

Psalm 103: Bless the LORD, O My Soul

1 Bless the LORD, O my soul: and all that is within me, bless his holy name.

2 Bless the LORD, O my soul, and forget not all his benefits:

3 Who forgiveth all thine iniquities; who healeth all thy diseases;

4 Who redeemeth thy life from destruction; who crowneth thee with lovingkindness and tender mercies;

5 Who satisfieth thy mouth with good things; so that thy youth is renewed like the eagle's.

6 The LORD executeth righteousness and judgment for all that are oppressed.

7 He made known his ways unto Moses, his acts unto the children of Israel.

8 The LORD is merciful and gracious, slow to anger, and plenteous in mercy.

9 He will not always chide: neither will he keep his anger for ever.

[10] He hath not dealt with us after our sins; nor rewarded us according to our iniquities.

[11] For as the heaven is high above the earth, so great is his mercy toward them that fear him.

[12] As far as the east is from the west, so far hath he removed our transgressions from us.

[13] Like as a father pitieth his children, so the LORD pitieth them that fear him.

[14] For he knoweth our frame; he remembereth that we are dust.

[15] As for man, his days are as grass: as a flower of the field, so he flourisheth.

[16] For the wind passeth over it, and it is gone; and the place thereof shall know it no more.

[17] But the mercy of the LORD is from everlasting to everlasting upon them that fear him, and his righteousness unto children's children;

[18] To such as keep his covenant, and to those that remember his commandments to do them.

[19] The LORD hath prepared his throne in the heavens; and his kingdom ruleth over all.

[20] Bless the LORD, ye his angels, that excel in strength, that do his commandments, hearkening unto the voice of his word.

[21] Bless ye the LORD, all ye his hosts; ye ministers of his, that do his pleasure.

[22] Bless the LORD, all his works in all places of his dominion: bless the LORD, O my soul.

Psalm 103: Bless the LORD, O My Soul

Psalm 103 is a great hymn to God's love and compassion toward his people. This Psalm begins with a call to praise the gracious Lord who bestows rich blessings upon his children. "Bless the LORD, O my soul: and all that is within me, bless his holy name."

We are called to remember all that God has done for us. His blessings range far and wide; they are exceedingly rich. "Bless the LORD, O my soul, and forget not all his benefits: Who forgiveth all thine iniquities; Who healeth all thy diseases; Who redeemeth thy life from destruction; Who crowneth thee with lovingkindness and tender mercies; Who satisfieth thy mouth with good things; so that thy youth is renewed like the eagle's."

God works salvation for his people as he removes our transgressions from us. Note the vivid description of this in verses 11-12. Also, note the tender compassion of our heavenly Father in verses 13-18. This Psalm is full of grace!

Psalm 103 ends with a call for all the angels and all of creation to praise our wondrous God. Read Luke 12:22-34 to see how Jesus describes the care and compassion our heavenly Father has for all his creatures, great and small. What comfort and reassurance do you find in these verses? How does Psalm 103 help you to understand the teaching and work of Christ?

Read this Psalm several times over the course of a few days. Let its message speak to your deepest needs. Reflect upon each verse.

"Bless the LORD, O my soul: and all that is within me, bless his holy name. Bless the LORD, O my soul, and forget not all his benefits."

Psalm 110: Thou Art a Priest For Ever

1   The LORD said unto my Lord, Sit thou at my right hand, until I make thine enemies thy footstool.

2   The LORD shall send the rod of thy strength out of Zion: rule thou in the midst of thine enemies.

3   Thy people shall be willing in the day of thy power, in the beauties of holiness from the womb of the morning: thou hast the dew of thy youth.

4   The LORD hath sworn, and will not repent, Thou art a priest for ever after the order of Melchizedek.

5   The Lord at thy right hand shall strike through kings in the day of his wrath.

6   He shall judge among the heathen, he shall fill the places with the dead bodies; he shall wound the heads over many countries.

7   He shall drink of the brook in the way: therefore shall he lift up the head.

Psalm 110: Thou Art a Priest For Ever

Psalm 110 is a Messianic Psalm that Jesus directly quotes and applies to himself.

David, the writer of this Psalm, confesses that the Messiah is his Lord. This Messiah will be a great King that God himself installs at his right hand (a reference to the ascension of Jesus). "The LORD said unto my Lord, Sit thou at my right hand, until I make thine enemies thy footstool."

The Messiah is also a great High Priest in the order of Melchizedek. "The LORD hath sworn, and will not repent, Thou art a priest for ever after the order of Melchizedek." The book of Hebrews tells us why such priesthood is superior to the priesthood of Aaron.

Read Mark 12:35-40 to see how the Son of David is also the Lord of David. Think about how Jesus is both God and man in one person. He is the true Son of God, but he is also true man. He is the child born of Mary in the town of Bethlehem, the town of David.

Then, read Hebrews 7:11-28 to discover how our High Priest would ultimately offer himself as the great and final sacrifice for the sins of the world.

Our Lord became flesh and blood to die for us on the cross. He suffers and dies as the Son of God.

Because our High Priest was both God and man, his atoning sacrifice pays the price for our sins. "Such a High Priest meets our needs. Therefore he is able to save completely those who come to God through him, because he always lives to intercede for them."

Reflect upon the fact that Christ is true God and true man in one person. How does this ensure our salvation? How does such a High Priest meet our needs?

Also, reflect upon the fact that the Risen and Ascended Lord is interceding for you right now before the Father in heaven. Pray to the Lord right now and share with him your burden. Receive his peace and blessing. Let his face shine upon you today.

Psalm 116: I Love the Lord

1 I love the LORD, because he hath heard my voice and my supplications.

2 Because he hath inclined his ear unto me, therefore will I call upon him as long as I live.

3 The sorrows of death compassed me, and the pains of hell gat hold upon me: I found trouble and sorrow.

4 Then called I upon the name of the LORD; O LORD, I beseech thee, deliver my soul.

5 Gracious is the LORD, and righteous; yea, our God is merciful.

6 The LORD preserveth the simple: I was brought low, and he helped me.

7 Return unto thy rest, O my soul; for the LORD hath dealt bountifully with thee.

8 For thou hast delivered my soul from death, mine eyes from tears, and my feet from falling.

⁹ I will walk before the LORD in the land of the living.

¹⁰ I believed, therefore have I spoken: I was greatly afflicted:

¹¹ I said in my haste, All men are liars.

¹² What shall I render unto the LORD for all his benefits toward me?

¹³ I will take the cup of salvation, and call upon the name of the LORD.

¹⁴ I will pay my vows unto the LORD now in the presence of all his people.

¹⁵ Precious in the sight of the LORD is the death of his saints.

¹⁶ O LORD, truly I am thy servant; I am thy servant, and the son of thine handmaid: thou hast loosed my bonds.

¹⁷ I will offer to thee the sacrifice of thanksgiving, and will call upon the name of the LORD.

¹⁸ I will pay my vows unto the LORD now in the presence of all his people,

19 In the courts of the LORD'S house, in the midst of thee, O Jerusalem. Praise ye the LORD.

Psalm 116: I Love the Lord

Note how this Psalm begins with the words, "I love the Lord." This entire Psalm is a great example of faith, love and devotion. We love God because he first loved us through his Son. God has rescued us through his mercy in Christ. "Gracious is the LORD, and righteous; yea, our God is merciful."

In our times of trouble, we cry out, "O Lord, save me!" and the Lord reaches out his hand to deliver us. "Then called I upon the name of the LORD; O LORD, I beseech thee, deliver my soul."

Read Matthew 14:22-36 to see how Jesus rescued Peter from drowning. This is a memorable picture of Christ helping us in our time of need. When we start sinking down with the burden that we carry, we need to simply cry out, "Lord, help me!"

"The LORD preserveth the simple: I was brought low, and he helped me."

"For thou hast delivered my soul from death, mine eyes from tears, and my feet from falling."

Psalm 116 deserves to be treasured as one of the great Psalms of faith and devotion to our Savior, Jesus Christ. Read this psalm aloud, carefully and slowly. Reflect upon each thought it expresses and repeat these words to yourself.

"The LORD preserveth the simple: I was brought low, and he helped me. Return unto thy rest, O my soul; for the LORD hath dealt bountifully with thee."

Psalm 118: The Stone the Builders Rejected

1 O give thanks unto the LORD; for he is good: because his mercy endureth for ever.

2 Let Israel now say, that his mercy endureth for ever.

3 Let the house of Aaron now say, that his mercy endureth for ever.

4 Let them now that fear the LORD say, that his mercy endureth for ever.

5 I called upon the LORD in distress: the LORD answered me, and set me in a large place.

6 The LORD is on my side; I will not fear: what can man do unto me?

7 The LORD taketh my part with them that help me: therefore shall I see my desire upon them that hate me.

8 It is better to trust in the LORD than to put confidence in man.

9 It is better to trust in the LORD than to put confidence in princes.

10 All nations compassed me about: but in the name of the LORD will I destroy them.

11 They compassed me about; yea, they compassed me about: but in the name of the LORD I will destroy them.

12 They compassed me about like bees; they are quenched as the fire of thorns: for in the name of the LORD I will destroy them.

13 Thou hast thrust sore at me that I might fall: but the LORD helped me.

14 The LORD is my strength and song, and is become my salvation.

15 The voice of rejoicing and salvation is in the tabernacles of the righteous: the right hand of the LORD doeth valiantly.

16 The right hand of the LORD is exalted: the right hand of the LORD doeth valiantly.

17 I shall not die, but live, and declare the works of the LORD.

¹⁸ The LORD hath chastened me sore: but he hath not given me over unto death.

¹⁹ Open to me the gates of righteousness: I will go into them, and I will praise the LORD:

²⁰ This gate of the LORD, into which the righteous shall enter.

²¹ I will praise thee: for thou hast heard me, and art become my salvation.

²² The stone which the builders refused is become the head stone of the corner.

²³ This is the LORD'S doing; it is marvellous in our eyes.

²⁴ This is the day which the LORD hath made; we will rejoice and be glad in it.

²⁵ Save now, I beseech thee, O LORD: O LORD, I beseech thee, send now prosperity.

²⁶ Blessed be he that cometh in the name of the LORD: we have blessed you out of the house of the LORD.

²⁷ God is the LORD, which hath showed us light: bind the sacrifice with cords, even unto the horns of the altar.

²⁸ Thou art my God, and I will praise thee: thou art my God, I will exalt thee.

²⁹ O give thanks unto the LORD; for he is good: for his mercy endureth for ever.

Psalm 118: The Stone the Builders Rejected

This is a longer Psalm that is often quoted by Jesus, his apostles and many Christians, even to this day.

This Psalm begins with a gripping prayer of thanksgiving for God's deliverance. "Thou hast thrust sore at me that I might fall: but the LORD helped me. The LORD is my strength and my song; he has become my salvation."

The second part of this Psalm features some of the most famous verses of the Bible. Verses 22-23 are a cryptic reference to the Messiah's rejection and ultimate triumph. Jesus quotes these verses as he defends and defines his saving work.

Read Mark 12:1-12 and note how our Lord uses Psalm 118 in the face of opposition and rejection. Remember that Jesus spoke these words only a few days before his crucifixion. He was the Stone the builders rejected.

Also noteworthy are verse 26, which becomes part of the Palm Sunday celebration (and our Communion service), and verses 24 & 29, which often appear in our liturgy, hymns, and other devotions. Write down and memorize all of these verses. Let them lead you to prayerful reflection upon God's gift of life and salvation.

Read again this Psalm. It was so important to Christ and his disciples. They saw God's salvation revealed through these words:

"The stone which the builders refused has become the head stone of the corner. This is the LORD'S doing; it is marvellous in our eyes."

"The LORD is my strength and song, and is become my salvation."

"The right hand of the LORD is exalted: the right hand of the LORD doeth valiantly."

"I shall not die, but live, and declare the works of the LORD."

"I will praise thee: for thou hast heard me, and art become my salvation."

"This is the day which the LORD hath made; we will rejoice and be glad in it."

Psalm 130: Out of the Depths

1 Out of the depths have I cried unto thee, O LORD.

2 Lord, hear my voice: let thine ears be attentive to the voice of my supplications.

3 If thou, LORD, shouldest mark iniquities, O Lord, who shall stand?

4 But there is forgiveness with thee, that thou mayest be feared.

5 I wait for the LORD, my soul doth wait, and in his word do I hope.

6 My soul waiteth for the Lord more than they that watch for the morning: I say, more than they that watch for the morning.

7 Let Israel hope in the LORD: for with the LORD there is mercy, and with him is plenteous redemption.

8 And he shall redeem Israel from all his iniquities.

Psalm 130: Out of the Depths

This Psalm is another cry for help and mercy. This short Psalm is a strong testimony of complete trust in the Lord. Even though we are sinners, God is gracious. God not only forgives our sins, but also remembers them no more. "If thou, LORD, shouldest mark iniquities, O Lord, who shall stand? But there is forgiveness with thee, that thou mayest be feared."

Notice how verses 5-6 express the patient hope of the believer. We put our hope in the Lord, no matter what our situation in life may be. We patiently wait for God's deliverance when we are in trouble. "I wait for the LORD, my soul doth wait, and in his word do I hope."

Read Luke 18:9-14 for the story of a man who prayed this message of Psalm 130. Notice the humble attitude of repentance and faith. Out of the depths of guilt and anguish, he simply prayed for God's mercy. "Lord, have mercy on me, a sinner."

Think about how you can use this Psalm in your daily prayers. Write out any verses that are meaningful for you and memorize them.

Psalm 136: His Mercy Endureth For Ever

1 O give thanks unto the LORD; for he is good: for his mercy endureth for ever.

2 O give thanks unto the God of gods: for his mercy endureth for ever.

3 O give thanks to the Lord of lords: for his mercy endureth for ever.

4 To him who alone doeth great wonders: for his mercy endureth for ever.

5 To him that by wisdom made the heavens: for his mercy endureth for ever.

6 To him that stretched out the earth above the waters: for his mercy endureth for ever.

7 To him that made great lights: for his mercy endureth for ever:

8 The sun to rule by day: for his mercy endureth for ever:

9 The moon and stars to rule by night: for his mercy endureth for ever.

¹⁰ To him that smote Egypt in their firstborn: for his mercy endureth for ever:

¹¹ And brought out Israel from among them: for his mercy endureth for ever:

¹² With a strong hand, and with a stretched out arm: for his mercy endureth for ever.

¹³ To him which divided the Red sea into parts: for his mercy endureth for ever:

¹⁴ And made Israel to pass through the midst of it: for his mercy endureth for ever:

¹⁵ But overthrew Pharaoh and his host in the Red sea: for his mercy endureth for ever.

¹⁶ To him which led his people through the wilderness: for his mercy endureth for ever.

¹⁷ To him which smote great kings: for his mercy endureth for ever:

¹⁸ And slew famous kings: for his mercy endureth for ever:

¹⁹ Sihon king of the Amorites: for his mercy endureth for ever:

20 And Og the king of Bashan: for his mercy endureth for ever:

21 And gave their land for an heritage: for his mercy endureth for ever:

22 Even an heritage unto Israel his servant: for his mercy endureth for ever.

23 Who remembered us in our low estate: for his mercy endureth for ever:

24 And hath redeemed us from our enemies: for his mercy endureth for ever.

25 Who giveth food to all flesh: for his mercy endureth for ever.

26 O give thanks unto the God of heaven: for his mercy endureth for ever.

Psalm 136: His Mercy Endureth For Ever

This is a liturgy of praise to God who is our Creator and Redeemer. Most likely, this Psalm was used in the worship service of the temple in Jerusalem. It would be perfect for a call and response type of chanting.

The first part, verses 1-9, speak of God as our Creator. God created the universe and the stars according to his wisdom and mercy. The gift of creation comes from our gracious Creator. "For his mercy endureth forever."

Verses 10-22 speak of God as Israel's Redeemer. Note the reference to the Exodus. That was the great salvation event of the Old Testament, which the people of Israel continually celebrated and remembered.

"And God brought out Israel from among them, with a strong hand and with a stretched out arm. He divided the Red sea into parts, and made Israel to pass through the midst of it. God overthrew Pharaoh and his host in the Red sea."

Verses 23-26 are a closing word of thanksgiving and praise. Try reading this entire Psalm aloud, and notice the rhythm, which helps you focus on the first part of each verse. Note the progression of thought.

See Revelation 7:9-17 for another example of a liturgy of praise to our Creator and Redeemer. Notice how even the angels will join us, as we praise the Triune God in heaven.

The Psalms remind us that God is worthy of praise, honor and joyful worship. Truly, "His mercy endureth for ever!"

Psalm 139: Thy Right Hand Shall Hold Me

1 O LORD, thou hast searched me, and known me.

2 Thou knowest my downsitting and mine uprising, thou understandest my thought afar off.

3 Thou compassest my path and my lying down, and art acquainted with all my ways.

4 For there is not a word in my tongue, but, lo, O LORD, thou knowest it altogether.

5 Thou hast beset me behind and before, and laid thine hand upon me.

6 Such knowledge is too wonderful for me; it is high, I cannot attain unto it.

7 Whither shall I go from thy spirit? or whither shall I flee from thy presence?

8 If I ascend up into heaven, thou art there: if I make my bed in hell, behold, thou art there.

9 If I take the wings of the morning, and dwell in the uttermost parts of the sea;

¹⁰ Even there shall thy hand lead me, and thy right hand shall hold me.

¹¹ If I say, Surely the darkness shall cover me; even the night shall be light about me.

¹² Yea, the darkness hideth not from thee; but the night shineth as the day: the darkness and the light are both alike to thee.

¹³ For thou hast possessed my reins: thou hast covered me in my mother's womb.

¹⁴ I will praise thee; for I am fearfully and wonderfully made: marvellous are thy works; and that my soul knoweth right well.

¹⁵ My substance was not hid from thee, when I was made in secret, and curiously wrought in the lowest parts of the earth.

¹⁶ Thine eyes did see my substance, yet being unperfect; and in thy book all my members were written, which in continuance were fashioned, when as yet there was none of them.

¹⁷ How precious also are thy thoughts unto me, O God! how great is the sum of them!

¹⁸ If I should count them, they are more in number than the sand: when I awake, I am still with thee.

¹⁹ Surely thou wilt slay the wicked, O God: depart from me therefore, ye bloody men.

²⁰ For they speak against thee wickedly, and thine enemies take thy name in vain.

²¹ Do not I hate them, O LORD, that hate thee? and am not I grieved with those that rise up against thee?

²² I hate them with perfect hatred: I count them mine enemies.

²³ Search me, O God, and know my heart: try me, and know my thoughts:

²⁴ And see if there be any wicked way in me, and lead me in the way everlasting.

Psalm 139: Thy Right Hand Shall Hold Me

Psalm 139 speaks of God's knowledge and presence. God is all-knowing and present everywhere. He knows our thoughts and desires, our actions and words, our attitudes and emotions. We cannot hide from God. He is present throughout the whole universe.

Psalm 139 applies these truths about God to comfort us in our daily life. God knows who we are and what we do. He knows we are sinners, and yet, he still loves and accepts us.

God forgives all of our sins in Christ. He is well aware of how we are frail sinners who struggle every day. God has mercy upon us as we struggle through this earthly life. His right hand is there to lift us up on eagles' wings.

Note verses 13-16 which speak of God's gift of life, which begins at conception. God created you to be special and unique. There is no one else in this entire world just like you. God made you to have a wonderful life.

"I will praise thee; for I am fearfully and wonderfully made: marvellous are thy works; and that my soul knoweth right well."

Read Ephesians 1:3-14 to discover how you were chosen in Christ before the creation of the world. Read this passage carefully to discover has God has chosen you in grace to be his very own. You have been redeemed by the blood of Christ and are sealed with the gift of the Holy Spirit.

"Praise be to the God and Father of our Lord Jesus Christ, who has blessed us in the heavenly realms with every spiritual blessing in Christ!"

Reflect upon and give thanks for God's gift of life and salvation in Jesus. The all-knowing and all-present God loves you and claims you as his very own. "How precious also are thy thoughts unto me, O God! how great is the sum of them!"

Psalm 143: Hear Me, O Lord

1 Hear my prayer, O LORD, give ear to my supplications: in thy faithfulness answer me, and in thy righteousness.

2 And enter not into judgment with thy servant: for in thy sight shall no man living be justified.

3 For the enemy hath persecuted my soul; he hath smitten my life down to the ground; he hath made me to dwell in darkness, as those that have been long dead.

4 Therefore is my spirit overwhelmed within me; my heart within me is desolate.

5 I remember the days of old; I meditate on all thy works; I muse on the work of thy hands.

6 I stretch forth my hands unto thee: my soul thirsteth after thee, as a thirsty land.
Selah

7 Hear me speedily, O LORD: my spirit faileth: hide not thy face from me, lest I be like unto them that go down into the pit.

8 Cause me to hear thy lovingkindness in the morning; for in thee do I trust: cause me to know the way wherein I should walk; for I lift up my soul unto thee.

9 Deliver me, O LORD, from mine enemies: I flee unto thee to hide me.

10 Teach me to do thy will; for thou art my God: thy spirit is good; lead me into the land of uprightness.

11 Quicken me, O LORD, for thy name's sake: for thy righteousness' sake bring my soul out of trouble.

12 And of thy mercy cut off mine enemies, and destroy all them that afflict my soul: for I am thy servant.

Psalm 143: Hear Me, O Lord

Psalm 143 is a prayer for God's help when you are in trouble. This is an honest confession of our frail mortality. Each of us needs God's help and deliverance. "Hear me speedily, O LORD: my spirit faileth: hide not thy face from me, lest I be like unto them that go down into the pit."

The "enemy" referred to can be any difficulty or heartache that causes great personal pain. Our problems and worries can become like a dangerous enemy that threatens to overwhelm us.

When this happens, God is our only hope for rescue. "I stretch forth my hands unto thee: my soul thirsteth after thee, as a thirsty land. Answer me quickly, O Lord; my spirit fails."

Read 2 Corinthians 12:1-10 to see how the apostle Paul had to deal with his enemy, a "thorn in the flesh." Note especially God's answer to him in verse 9. Write this answer down on a card and memorize it. Also, reflect upon what St. Paul says in verse 10: "When I am weak, God is strong."

Use Psalm 143 as a prayer when you are in trouble or struggling with depression. Open your heart to God and remember that your Creator loves you. He will help you in your time of need.

Just be strong and keep the faith. Keep looking to Christ and his grace. "My grace is sufficient for you and my power is made perfect in weakness." Amen!

Psalm 145: I Will Extol Thee, My God

1 I will extol thee, my God, O king; and I will bless thy name for ever and ever.

2 Every day will I bless thee; and I will praise thy name for ever and ever.

3 Great is the LORD, and greatly to be praised; and his greatness is unsearchable.

4 One generation shall praise thy works to another, and shall declare thy mighty acts.

5 I will speak of the glorious honour of thy majesty, and of thy wondrous works.

6 And men shall speak of the might of thy terrible acts: and I will declare thy greatness.

7 They shall abundantly utter the memory of thy great goodness, and shall sing of thy righteousness.

8 The LORD is gracious, and full of compassion; slow to anger, and of great mercy.

9 The LORD is good to all: and his tender mercies are over all his works.

¹⁰ All thy works shall praise thee, O LORD; and thy saints shall bless thee.

¹¹ They shall speak of the glory of thy kingdom, and talk of thy power;

¹² To make known to the sons of men his mighty acts, and the glorious majesty of his kingdom.

¹³ Thy kingdom is an everlasting kingdom, and thy dominion endureth throughout all generations.

¹⁴ The LORD upholdeth all that fall, and raiseth up all those that be bowed down.

¹⁵ The eyes of all wait upon thee; and thou givest them their meat in due season.

¹⁶ Thou openest thine hand, and satisfiest the desire of every living thing.

¹⁷ The LORD is righteous in all his ways, and holy in all his works.

¹⁸ The LORD is nigh unto all them that call upon him, to all that call upon him in truth.

¹⁹ He will fulfil the desire of them that fear him: he also will hear their cry, and will save them.

²⁰ The LORD preserveth all them that love him: but all the wicked will he destroy.

²¹ My mouth shall speak the praise of the LORD: and let all flesh bless his holy name for ever and ever.

Psalm 145: I Will Extol Thee, My God

Psalm 145 is a Psalm of praise to God. We are called to praise God for his greatness and majesty. His mighty acts display his goodness and grace. "I will extol thee, my God, O king; and I will bless thy name for ever and ever. Every day will I bless thee; and I will praise thy name for ever and ever."

Note the classic description of God in verses 8-9. "The LORD is gracious, and full of compassion; slow to anger, and of great mercy. The LORD is good to all: and his tender mercies are over all his works."

Read 1 Corinthians 1:1-9 for another description of God's faithfulness to his saints. We have been enriched in every way so that we can also praise our gracious God for his gift of salvation in Christ.

St. Paul's thanksgiving to God for the faith of the Corinthians echoes the call of Psalm 145.

"The LORD is nigh unto all them that call upon him, to all that call upon him in truth."

"Great is the LORD, and greatly to be praised; and his greatness is unsearchable."

Read this Psalm again and notice how carefully it is structured. The last verse truly summarizes how we should use all the Psalms.

Let us continually give praise to our God for his faithfulness and grace.

"My mouth shall speak the praise of the LORD: and let all flesh bless his holy name for ever and ever." Amen!

Here's a bonus sermon
from the book, No More Tears:

THE LORD IS MY SHEPHERD: Psalm 23:1-6

A shepherd had 100 sheep in his flock. One evening, he counted them as they came back home through the gate of the sheep pen. Only 99 were there! One was missing. It must have been separated from the flock and lost in the woods.

At once, the shepherd closed the gate and left his helpers to watch over the flock. He had to find that lost sheep before some wolf could get to her.

He hurried back to the places where the flock had been that day. He called the sheep's name repeatedly. For a while, the shepherd heard nothing. Again and again, he called.

At last, he heard a weak cry. Before long, he found the sheep, all tangled up in some bushes. He gently pulled her out, but found she could not walk. She had hurt her leg. Therefore, he picked her up, and carried her home in his arms.

This shepherd is someone we all know. It is our Lord Jesus Christ. We are his sheep, and sometimes we get lost, too. We get separated from God's flock. We go down the wrong path. We get confused and lose our way. We get hurt.

But today our Shepherd calls us back. He searches for us and calls us by name. He finds us and binds up our wounds. And this Shepherd rejoices over all his sheep.

That is what makes Psalm 23 so powerful and special. Psalm 23 is the most beloved of all the Psalms. And it begins by saying, "The Lord is my Shepherd; I shall not want."

That is quite a statement, isn't it? Think about it. Our Psalm is actually saying, "Since the Lord is my Shepherd, I will never lack a thing in my life. I shall not want."

How can that be true? It often feels like there are many things lacking in our life. It often seems like we do suffer want. Our life feels empty and hollow. There is so much that is missing in our life. How can Psalm 23 say such a thing?

But perhaps what is missing in our life is faith. We lack a simple trust in God's goodness and grace. That's why our spiritual life is so shaky and uncertain. Such a lack of faith leads to endless doubts and fears.

The simple truth is we have such a hard time believing what God says. That is why we struggle so much in our spiritual life. It might even reach a point where we cry out, "Lord, help me! Increase my faith! Help me to trust in you. Show me how to get rid of my doubts and fears."

Today, the Shepherd calls out to his lost sheep. He says, "I am the Good Shepherd. I know my sheep and my sheep know me. And I lay down my life for my sheep."

Our Shepherd knows us and he knows our situation. He knows our faith is weak and uncertain. The Shepherd is well aware of the condition of all of his sheep. And he knows that we are hurting inside. We feel lost and all alone.

That is why he says, "Listen to my voice when I call to you. Hear my Word! Listen to what I say and you will have all that you need."

Our Shepherd wants to lead us to the green pastures of his Word. He wants to bring us once again to the still waters of Holy Baptism. He seeks to restore our soul through the power of Holy Communion.

Today, our Lord leads us down the path of his cross and resurrection. He forgives our sins for his name's sake. He anoints our head with the oil of grace. Our cup of blessing just overflows, and we once again discover what we really need in this life.

Our Shepherd feeds us with his Word and Sacraments. That is why worship is so important. At worship, we hear the voice of the Shepherd who searches for us. He calls to us. He feeds our hungry heart. He restores our soul. He bestows his gift of forgiveness.

The Lord nourishes us through his Word and Sacraments, and in this way, faith is created and strengthened. Our spiritual hunger is satisfied. Our doubts and fears now begin to fade away. We receive a spiritual healing. Our wounds are bound up and we are restored.

Jesus says, "I am the Good Shepherd. My sheep listen to my voice. I know them and they follow me. I give them eternal life. And my sheep shall never perish; no one can snatch them out of my hand."

Our Shepherd promises to guide us through this life. He goes ahead of us and protects us every step of the way. He says, "Come, follow me! I will show you the way to go." When the Lord steps into your life, you discover that you do have everything you need.

Now, you can joyfully confess, "The Lord Jesus Christ is my shepherd; I shall not want. He makes me lie down in green pastures. He leads me beside the still waters. He restores my soul; he leads me in the paths of righteousness for his name's sake. Even though I walk through the valley of the shadow of death, I will fear no evil; for you, O Lord Jesus, are with me, your rod and staff they comfort me."

Yes, even if we walk through the deepest valley, we have everything we need. Even in the darkest of times, Christ is with us. You are safe in the loving arms of the Good Shepherd.

That is important to remember when you go through those tough times. Life is often filled with the dark valleys, low points, and difficult days. We all struggle with our pain and hurts. We all experience depression, sadness and grief. Perhaps you are going through such a deep, dark valley right now in your life.

"But even if I walk through the valley of the shadow of death, I will fear no evil; for the Lord Jesus Christ is with me. His cross and resurrection, they comfort me. In times of trouble, I turn to my Savior. The Lord is my Shepherd; I shall not want!"

Always remember this: Christ laid down his life for you. That's how much he loves you. Christ was thinking of you when he died on that cross. He was thinking of you when he laid down his life. That's why you belong to him. You are his sheep, his lamb.

The Good Shepherd now calls to you. Can you hear him? He is saying, "Come on and follow me! I will walk with you though those valleys that lie ahead. Together, we can make it. I will bless you with my presence. I will feed you with my Word and Sacraments. I will strengthen your faith and give you all you need."

That is the promise that the Lord Jesus makes to all of us. He gives us his Word. He prepares the table of his Supper for us. He anoints our head with the oil of baptismal grace. Our cup of blessing just overflows!

We now have that certainty of knowing that God's goodness and mercy will follow us all the days of our life. The Good Shepherd leads us through our earthly journey, and then, he leads us all the way home, where we shall dwell in the house of the Lord forever. Amen!

ABOUT THE AUTHOR:

Volker Heide graduated from the United States Merchant Marine Academy in Kings Point, New York in 1982. (B.S., Nautical Science) and worked in the offshore oil industry. He graduated from Concordia Seminary in St. Louis, Missouri in 1990. (M.Div., New Testament Theology).

He has been a parish pastor in the Lutheran Church – Missouri Synod for almost 30 years, and has served churches in Mississippi and Connecticut. He is married to his wife, Ellen, and they have two daughters, Melissa and Kristen.

38280279R00084

Made in the USA
Middletown, DE
07 March 2019